Souled Out

The Secrets on Westside

"Reclaiming life from a journey of grief, deception, and lecherous affairs."

Written by:

Inetta Lowery

Edited, Formatted, Designed & Published

by

Wade Christian Publishing LLC

www.wadepublishers.com

info@wadepublishers.com

Souled Out: The Secrets on Westside

Written by Inetta Lowery

Paperback ISBN: 979-8-9864810-3-6

E-Book ISBN: 979-8-9864810-4-3

Dedication

This book is first dedicated to my late Grandmother, Mary. You were the first ever to see the Writer and the Speaker in me. As a little girl sitting in your lap, you always told me that I had these unique gifts. I could not see it then. I hope my gifts please your spirit. I am forever grateful that you helped me find my most authentic voice.

To my Mother, I am your namesake, and I hold that torch in its highest regard. I am most likely your biggest headache, also. Hence, my gratitude for you being strong-armed when I needed your firmness. I am even more thankful for your softness at just the right times. You have laid the platform. You are the original Prototype. You are always loving (in your own way) and support me. You have never allowed me to give up on myself.

I also dedicate this book to my one and only sweetheart daughter, Khey. Everything I do is for you. These words will be part of my legacy because of your push. If only you knew how much you have made me a better person with your unconditional love, tenacity, and strength. You inspire me, and my gratitude is immeasurable. In the end, you are eternally my greatest accomplishment.

Much Love.

Epigraph

"The hearts of the bereaved are harbored in sorrow until the souls of our loved ones ascend at first light to meet the face of the sun."

-Composed by Inetta Lowery

Table of Contents

Introduction

I can remember us dancing in the aisles of the Kem concert as he sang "Promise to Love." You wore all black, and scents of your Dior cologne teased the warm, moist depths of my feminine wiles. So much love and euphoria were in the air that I could taste it. I treasure this moment more than you will ever know. Then, life happens, unapologetically and without notice.

I want to share with you my personal story of betrayal, heartbreak, and grief-stricken. I birthed this memoir to bring comfort and uplift others who felt there was no way back from pain. Today, I open myself up to you and recount how I once died and was resurrected.

Here is how my journey goes…

"It takes sadness to know what happiness is. Noise to appreciate silence & absence to value presence."

—Unknown

Prologue

As I laid down to go to sleep, I ran my fingers over the band that encircled my ring finger. I had said Yes, and I would soon be changing my last name. A chance meeting almost a year ago had led me to the love of my life. Laying in my bed as I drifted off to sleep, I knew not too many more nights would end like this. The wedding plans were already in motion, and I basically spent more time at his house than I did my own. Thoughts about upcoming wedding plans came into my mind as I drifted off to sleep, not knowing that my life would be turned upside down in hours.

It was an early Spring morning circa March 2015. I was soundly asleep in bed. My phone rang with a voice on the other end asking if I had spoken to you. Meanwhile, I thought you were asleep and called your phone. The voicemail picked up quickly. Hanging up, I slipped back into sleep, and I did not think any more of it.

Later, I heard a faint, haunting knock at my front door that jarred me awake. Hysterically, I jumped up and allowed my eyes to adjust to the light in my bedroom. It was at the break of dawn's first light. Home alone, I immediately scrambled off the bed and grabbed my gun. It's now unlocked and loaded. Carefully, I approached the door and asked who was there. My heart buffeted as if it would beat right out of my bosom.

I hear the unfamiliar and dispirited voice of a very slender yet svelte framed woman from the other side. She was accompanied by a more seasoned and cavalier gentleman standing behind her. With my gun still at my side and rubbing the sleep from my eyes, I reluctantly opened the door to invite them in.

They came in and I closed the door. From the look they had in their eyes, I knew something wasn't good. I certainly didn't know my world was about to be ripped to pieces.

She wasted no time telling me that the love of my life had met his fate. He was tragically killed. My legs weakened, and my body became powerless as I fell back into the wall screaming towards Heaven. God, please! Do not let this be true!

My pajamas were all bedraggled and soaking wet from the tears streaming down my face. The hurt was extremely pressing and heavy. I was breathless and somewhat paralyzed. This was the moment I had also died. I wanted someone to shake me and tell me it was all a terrible dream, but no one did.

The memoir you're about to read is about how I went from planning a wedding to attending a funeral in one night. I felt like my life had also been ripped from me, and I didn't think I would survive. This book tells all about how I was rebuilt into the woman that I am today and how I gained my life back through God's Word. This was my journey, and this is my truth. These were secrets meant to be left on the Westside. Come and take this journey with me.

Psalm 34:18

"The Lord is close to the brokenhearted and saves those who are crushed in spirit."

Chapter 1: At First Light

For months, I literally walked around like I was auditioning for a part in a horror movie. I was a zombie. During the day, I would carry on as if everything were normal. I acted as if I was coping. I put on the face that everyone expected me to have on. The strong, Black woman persona who was supposed to have everything together. Nothing was to unnerve me.

But ultimately, I was avoiding interactions with other people. I only spoke or held conversations when it was necessary. I just wanted to be invisible and heal in peace.

When night fell, so did the mask. I was alone with my thoughts, and I wasn't okay. I could then let all my feelings out without fear of persecution. I cried all evening and night from when I reached the concrete of my driveway. I was hurting in ways that I never thought that I would. How do you go from planning a wedding to planning a funeral? How do you bounce back from something like this?

No one wanted to acknowledge my truth or hear my side. The influx of lies and fabricated stories surrounding your death was unbelievable. Ugh! The audacity of those bitches! I was treated in ways that made me shut everyone out.

As the days lingered, I slept on my leather Chesterfield with all the lights on in the house. I couldn't bear returning to my room where my love and I had slept. The pain was getting the best of me. Depression from the grief began to fester deep within me like a nasty sore. I would go days without eating, which prompted a large amount of unhealthy weight loss. My skin darkened, and my hair was thinning. Taking showers or even brushing my teeth took a perceptible effort. There was no life left in me; it was as if I was dead. I functioned just enough to get through my day and back to my Chesterfield to drown in the sea of grief and depression that was slowly taking over my life.

My depression went on for months. Then, one morning as I was attempting to get dressed, a beam of sunlight flooded my bedroom, causing my eyes to catch a glimpse of myself in the dresser mirror. I could no longer avoid it. Staring back at me was only the capsule of what used to be a buoyantly and spiritedly young Woman.

I didn't recognize who the person was looking back at me. My hands flew to my face, and at that moment, I realized it was me. I had allowed grief and depression to suck the very life out of me.

After seeing this image ogling back at me, I cried out with everything in me. "Help me! Help me, Lord! I am empty and weakened. I am broken. You said you would never leave me." Through all my yearnings, this time was different. It was as though I felt strength coming from within.

The tears streaming down my face were now draining the energy from me, but I felt something else leaving me, depression. It was as with each tear, the depression cloud had lifted its overcast. From that moment on, I knew God would be the only one who could bring me back. But how?

Psalm 34:18

"The Lord is close to the brokenhearted and saves those who are crushed in spirit."

Chapter 2: The Process

Going forward each night, I found a Bible verse to meditate on before going to sleep. I had discovered how God's words gave me consolation. I clearly heard His voice say, "I am near. Hang on to My words in your time of tragedy."

I was overwhelmed with despondency. I was hopelessly suffocating from the pits of grief and depression. Yet, the spirit of the Lord spoke, asking me to trust and allow Him to come in. He promised to restore all my hope and save my life. Every day had its struggle, but God's Word provided the hope I needed to get through.

Psalm 71:20
"Though you have made me see troubles, many and bitter, you will restore my life again: from the depths of the earth, you will again bring me up."

With each pressing day, I dug deeper into God's promise in my living room. I kept telling myself that through all the hurt, all the painful crying out, and insomniac nights, my Father knew exactly what I needed to heal. He was listening to my pain-filled heart. God is the air that I breathe, and I trust His faithfulness. He still lives within me. My thoughts are more precise and vivid now. The cloud that dimmed my light began to lift, and my vision became clear.

From that point, I began to deepen my relationship with my Father. His Words became the anchor in my life. I understood that even through a storm, He embraced me.

God hears my shallow and faint whispers as I come to Him often in secret despair. The things that once bound me in grief became part of my healing. The chesterfield that I had slept on for months had become the armor of God. My living room was now being declared my **War Room**.

On the sofa, I hugged an old blanket tightly and repeatedly uttered Bible verses until I fell asleep. It doubled as a prayer cloth when fighting back the tears. God's Word was my treatment plan. No doctor or counselor could prescribe any medicine better than the healing spirit of Jesus Christ. How do I know? Because I have tried it. Formal counseling just did not work for me. The counselor gave me a few sympathetic words regarding my loss and handed me a bill. I don't even recall her ever giving me any eye contact during the sessions. Maybe a head nod here or there. I called it the scientific approach. But I needed something more profound and supernatural.

Each day after work, I gathered myself in the War Room to speak with God. I sat in a slumped, Indian-style position on the floor, where I solemnly prayed to survive my troubles. I asked, "What is your plan for me now, God?" The affliction of my grief and depression have now cut far below the surface skin.

With each passing day, the woman I once was, was slowly returning. The bounce back was natural, but I was determined to come back even better and stronger than before. I had to keep fighting with everything that I had in me. It was a new fight now, with the opponent being me against me. I now realized that I was fighting for the life that God wanted me to have all along. He wanted me to have that relationship with Him because it is only through Him that I could be made entirely whole again.

Chapter 2 Questions

1. What are the things you feel are trying to overtake you in your life?

2. Have you given your issues over to God and left them with Him?

3. Do you think that you need a significant other to feel complete?

4. Have you sought God for the plan and purpose of your life?

Faith Confession:

I am the head and not the tail; above only and never beneath. I am fearfully and wonderfully made and because you created me and everything you created was good. I am good and complete with you.

Jeremiah 29:11

"For I know the plans I have for you, declares the Lord. Plans to prosper you and not to harm you. Plans to give you hope and a future."

Chapter 3: His Ways Aren't Our Ways

It is now a hot and humid morning on June 29th. A couple of months have now gone by since my fiancé's passing. I received a call from my Mother, which is normal. We spoke several times daily, so I was not alarmed. She was getting ready to start her day. Mom usually cuts right through the chase and lays it on the line. Picture a short, red-haired woman with a very expressive point of view, usually with her hands on her hips. She's not the emotional type, to say the least.

Today, she begins her colloquy conversation by saying, "Don't talk. I just need you to listen." I am bracing myself and thinking, "Please God, no more bad news." She says, "I just want you to know how much I love you. I know things about you that only a Mother or God himself could know."

At this point, I am quietly in tears on the other end of the phone as I listen. She goes on to say, "You're still grieving very hard. I understand that is the price you pay when losing someone you love with all your heart. Even God knows what it is like to feel sorrow and loss. And it is okay for you to cry sometimes. Death changes a person until you come to terms with acceptance. Just continue to let the Lord guide you and hold on for healing and strength. Don't give up on yourself or life."

John 11:35
"Jesus wept."

Until now, I had never perceived how many branches could sprout from the tree of grief and depression. I was alone all the time and needed to focus on healing my emotional wounds and consciousness. Grief shows you how significant it is to spend valuable time with loved ones while you still have them.

I now ate alone, shopped alone, went to church alone; I was alone all the time. I no longer had a wedding to look forward to. Holidays were the most challenging, and most emotionally draining days. I became angry, knowing I had to allow myself to cope with these feelings. Yet, I heard God's voice again, "Don't give up now. Your breakthrough is near. Stand in your light."

John 14:27
"Peace I leave with you; my peace I give to you. I do not give to you as the world gives. Do not let your heart be troubled, and do not be afraid."

I prayed consistently throughout my days and nights. Finally, I was beginning to find a vibration of love, peace, and harmony where there was once disparity. Just like a baby and yielding my light, God nurtured me. My Father had protected me from further grief and gloominess. He spoon-fed into my soul, strengthened me in sadness, and gave me hope.

1 Peter 5:7
Cast all your anxiety on Him because He cares for you.

God is a healer. A spiritual awakening was erupting from a sacred mountain of blessings. It was time to tame the winds, seek ascension and cover all the festering wounds. I had shown God my wounds so that He may cleanse them in His mercy. Death is a spiritual journey that must be dealt with through God. Allow your spiritual consciousness to evolve and never waver in faith. Things will get better.

Psalm 119:50
"My comfort in my suffering is this: Your promise
preserves my life."

Philippians 4:6
"Do not be anxious about anything, but in every
situation, by prayer and petition, with thanksgiving:
present your requests to God."

Everything reminded me of him, my Love. I can affectionately remember being outside one day in a parking lot. I was looking for a necklace I had dropped somewhere in my car. I had gotten out to open the trunk, where I continued my search. Suddenly, I stopped what I was doing to look up and around me. I was sure that I had smelled the scent of his cologne. I looked around again, only to find no one else in sight.

I slowly looked down at my feet, where a feather lay fallen. My heart tells me that he was there, in the afterlife. He was making sure that I was doing alright, like he always did. My heart smiled, but my stomach dropped. I felt a hollow feeling like that of when you reach the lowest dip in a roller coaster ride at the county fair. Now, everyone will not fathom what it will take for you to heal, or how long it will take. Just do what is best for you and hold on to God's unchanging hands. Trust in His faithfulness for healing and guidance.

Psalm 147:3
"He heals the brokenhearted and binds up their
wounds."

With all my lumps and bruises, I am most grateful that God's hands are in everything I do. He chooses when we are born and when we die. During these times, such as grief and sorrow, we learn who is truly in control. Another day's journey of burdens had passed, and I made it through.

Chapter 4: Tangled Webs

Days, weeks, and even months went by when I was alone to battle and contemplate over my thoughts. I have since replayed every gesture and reflected on every word said to me when learning of his death. Now that I am stronger, I can justly say this is the point where I break the silence about when embitterment struck. However, I will attempt to be fleeting in my saltiness out of respect.

I remember packing my things to move from the home in banana boxes that my friend's husband picked up at a local grocery store nearby. This was not even a full day after the homegoing ceremony and burial. With my heart cracked open came tears of constraint. I had seen where his family members had been rifling through my personal belongings without permission as they scrambled to find access to bank accounts and other assets.

My grief did not allow me to speak or utter a word then. As I packed my boxes to reside at my previous home, the eyes of a scorpion were on my back. My body tightened, and I was hotter than the 38 Special we kept underneath our mattress. I was underwhelmed by all the mockery, flippancy, and downright audacious behaviors. Bougie scammers from the lake were in on the plot too. Ugh! I grind my teeth as I write this.

Everything that was given to me by my fiancé was taken away, given away, or sold without a drop of consideration. They even dared to ask me to return my engagement ring. However, that was not going to happen. After everything that was taken from me, the ring that symbolized the love that we shared was not going to be taken away from me. It was all I had.

I refused to give my ring back to them. They started to talk about me and scandalize my name. After everything that was done to me, and being told of his death, no one stood by me as he would have done. They tried to make me feel as though I should have been in the casket instead. While packing my belongings in those banana boxes, I took verbal abuse, snide remarks, and backward comments.

Indubitably, God Himself stepped down from the clouds on this day to personally secure me. Otherwise, I may have blacked out in a rage and choked the nearest neck for being so malicious and scandalizing my good name. They really tried to break me. But I am thankful that I know God, and He lives within me because it was Him that kept me that day from acting as I really wanted to. During all of that, I reminded myself that they could never erase the love that we once shared. At the end of the day, your time and purpose were well served. Being selfish, it took a long time for me to be able to say or accept this.

Ephesians 4:26-27
"26-In your anger, do not sin. Do not let the sun go down while you are still angry. 27-And, do not give the Devil a foothold."

You see, the Devil comes in many forms. On that day, I felt wholehearted that he took full form and hastily stared me in my eyes. Yet, God subtly reminds me that it is a path for me. "Just slow down, and I will order your steps. You will not see it now. Your blessings are being prepared in this process."

Breathe in, breathe out. Yes, I do understand that others were grieving also. Everyone grieves in their own way, and I reverence that. Just allow me to be obvious. I am unapologetic for the unbridled feelings I had chained down to protect others who were stepping all over me. A few wretches had kicked me when I was down at my lowest. However, one day, they all will see judgment and must face the consequences of their actions, by His stripes.

Galatians 6:7
"Do not be deceived. God cannot be mocked.
Whatever a man sows, he will reap in return."

We can all proclaim that God gives us obstacles and challenges in life, putting us closer to our divine purpose—showing us our purpose and what He thinks of us. In a situation where I was unsteady, I prayed for strength. God then gave me a mirror. I saw several reflections of myself. He revealed a woman who was broken, exasperated, and grim. In His name, the last reflection of myself showed me an image of a woman being healed. Her light was shining, and restoration was in sight again. A breakthrough was in the making.

This mirror showed me a vision of a woman that God had made a promise over her life. He was executing His prophecy. Instead of asking Him how I should attack the opposition, I inquired of God for direction in a battle I was not supposed to be in. He gave me a new identity and mapped my path. God have made me a conqueror.

Chapter 5: The Funeral

Sitting there grieving on the floor next to your casket was brutal. I had no special time with you alone. The moments I could take in were inconsiderately interrupted by your dearest Mother as she asked me to remove myself from the room as your offspring arrived with your former Wife. She rode VIP to the celebration sitting next to your beloved Mother in the first family car. While I, your fiancée, rode shotgun in the last car traveling to the church. But, let me halt and count my many blessings.

Meanwhile, I was preparing myself for your life's celebration. However, it did not feel that way. They begrudgingly carried on treating me as an insignificant person. I just let it pass, although something intense began to wither inside me as speakers were called to the podium to say words of blessings over you. My peripheral view picked up piercing eyes like those of a crow. They were staring me down as if I should not have been there. They also returned all the flowers I had purchased for your gravesite.

Many nights, I felt the warmth of his faint kisses on my cheeks while I slept. I heard the whispers of him saying my name, and woke up each morning consistently at 3:16 am. This was not easy. Yes, the numbers are relevant. I was not nurtured for this type of pain. But dear God, I felt your embrace. He had finished running his course, and I shall not endure alone.

Thank you, God, for allowing your heartbroken, angry daughter to go through a storm of chaos that handicapped me and made me call out for you.

Exodus 14:14

"The Lord will fight for you. You need only to be still."

Chapter 6: God Kept Me

Peace be still. Through grief, pain, and persecution, I remained sane. Behind the scenes, You were at work and heard my prayers. Tears were in the ground watering a seed; then took root. The tide of my battle was beginning to turn away and subside. The giant was being defeated, and the buzzards were fed the remains. I waited patiently in expectancy of favor as You dispatched Your angels to come to my rescue. I believe that You will take me to the fullness of my destiny.

Like Moses, God granted me a rod when pain and fear had their foot on my neck. I could not breathe. Yet, I fought my way out of the soil like a mighty Oak tree, rooted from an acorn seed. Although not on my time clock, I was transformed into a champion of grace. My rod saved me when the storm was intense, lightning was sharp, and winds were gushing.

Death! Why did you come here?! I went from planning a wedding to passing out in my living room. Now, staring down at you in a coffin of a cold, dark funeral home. As others arrived for your viewing, I moved to a squat on the floor nearby. I heard people speak reflections of you, then fade away in the background after paying their respects.
It all seemed like a dream. Yes! We laughed, joked, and shared fond memories of you. But my heart still aches for your love, my skin still aches for your touch and presence. Your presence was and is still missed. After the funeral, I moved back into my place. I tried hard to return to the life I had known before you. However, it was easier said than done.

"God can restore what is broken and change it into something amazing. All you need is faith."

There were countless insomniac nights of walking the floor until my feet were swollen and tender to the touch. My heart had periods of guilt where I wished I could have changed the outcome. Many days, depression overwhelmed me with too much exhaustion to eat a meal or take a shower. Oh! Let us not forget the long conversations with myself because no one else was around to listen.

I felt like Humpy Dumpty. I had fallen off the wall, and no one could put me back together again. I had a great fall; I had rolled down the hill with no one to put me back together. It was as though I was broken beyond repair. I tried to fight, walk with my head held high, remembering the love that we shared, to only have that thrown in my face. The people who were around me didn't want to see the broken side of me. The side that was barely holding onto life. So, I tried to walk like everything was together and that I had it together, but that was far from the truth.

Moving through life without you was something I had become ill-equipped for. While we are born to die one day, it was so hard to comprehend why your life ended right before ours together could start. It is crazy how fast we meshed together, and it seemed as though we were made for each other. Going through life with you became great. Yes, we had our obstacles, as all relationships do, and the ability to grow through them.

Tears fall when I think about what we had together. Life is now different after that night. It was hard and overwhelming to relearn how to navigate life without him.

Remember this.

The anointing of God is over your life. His promises are precise and consistent. Be humbled and grateful for each second with your loved ones. We could not get through life's trials and Satan's adversaries without the armor of God. We are protected. So, take a deep breath and tap into your ocean-sized potential.

Colossians 3:14

And over all these virtues put on love, which binds them all together in perfect unity.

Chapter 7: The Story

This was not part of the plan at all, Beloved. Just reflecting on the nights, we stayed up late talking about how we met. Head over heels, I believed it was a fairytale love story. Not many people can say they have met the love of their life at their front doorstep.

You had only been home from a tour of duty in Afghanistan for a few weeks, and adjusting to living back in the South. On this day, one of my closest friends was visiting me at home like normal. We were laughing and talking trash as usual. His phone then rang, and it was you on the other end needing to pick up something. I gave my permission for you to come through and get it. I now believe it was a setup so we could meet.

I never expected us to meet again or even thought about it. Then, I saw you at the company where I worked, and you asked for my number in your Mother's presence. Although, I bashfully hesitated. It was from that point on we were inseparable. Hmmm... How can I describe you? I loved your dark chocolate, brown skin. You were bowlegged and had a small frame. The most attractive thing about you was your intelligence. You were smart to choose a woman like me (insider). LOL.

As time went on, our friendship grew into an undeniable love. You proposed to me after three treasured months of dating. I did not accept due to learning you were coming out of a long-term relationship not very long before we met. Initially, you had deceived me about your status and had false intentions.

There were people dragging my name through the mud. I spared you from the embarrassment you handed me, and from the butt whooping you would have endured if God were not still working with me. Trust me, all you gossipers earned having me place both my feet where the sun does not shine! It was never I who was being manipulative. My heart was pure, and my intentions were genuine.

Whew! I had to get that off my chest. Now, back to you, my Love. Our meeting was inevitably in God's plan. It was no coincidence nor a fluke accident. God has a sense of humor that needs to play out in its divine way. There were lessons to be learned from this encounter.

You caught me off guard in my own little world. I was minding my precious business, going to work every day, and trying to put my daughter through college. I was content in my singleness. But your chase was relentless, and you did not stop until your mission was accomplished—a true Devil Dog after my own heart.

The first time you came over alone, you brought a bottle of Moet & Chandon Imperial. You gave me some Chanel perfume, with a pack of peanut M&Ms, as a joke. You were always quite the Comedian.

Nonetheless, from the long walks in the neighborhood, to the Boot Camp workouts, you had me attempt, from the spontaneous weekend getaways on the Harley Davidson, to attending church service or hanging at the lake, it did not matter the time or day we were together.

The night before your departure, you and I had a very emotional conversation earlier that evening, as most couples do. I was also not feeling well and decided it would be best to stay at my own home that night. So, I did just that. When I got there, I cleaned a little to compose myself. Afterward, I took a warm shower and went to bed with the TV watching over me.

Surprisingly, I realized you had not called to check on me as you usually would. I thought you had fallen asleep due to taking your normal OTC sleep supplement. Then, I found out you were inanimate. Ugh... The way I was told about your passing was insensible, slick, and tasteless. I would not have done that to even a rabid dog.

Later, malicious innuendos began disseminating that I was the reason for your demise. My name was being denounced by people saying defamatory things about me and cultivating pits of lies. I would enter a room, and people would snarf at me and turn their backs not to have to fancy a conversation with me. It was like being isolated in a pandemic. Even at your funerary, people were chuckling and smirking. I was belittled down to a strumpet and ridiculed as a savage. They mainly your beloved kindred, were vicious attackers.

It is jocular how you had always warned me about them. I can now wholly comprehend all the upheaval you experienced during juvenility. I am marveled at those whose behaviors encompass such great ignorance and occult mannerisms. My prayer is for their repentance or resurgence of the good Lord's spirit into their dark hearts.

In the final analysis of it all, I was fundamentally exposed to the hate-filled spirits you riddled about. I was not prepared because I wanted you to be wrong or over exaggerating. I am left in a state of apathy and inadequacy. But still, I believe in the timing of God, and I know that death does not end love. The cascading tears down my face are reflective of those which flood my heart. Nonetheless, I do not walk alone. This mountain of heaviness will be moved because God is my refuge.

As I reminisce, it is understood we had a bond like no other. Not even the slovenly "Nurse Fe" turning tricks in her slutty boudoir could extinguish the fire that was lit. Yes, I knew about it and chuckled with cynicism. And yes, I also knew about the house calls made to Mommy Dearest. You see, this whole time, I was protecting your honor while my character took an unnecessary drubbing in your expiration. I sheltered the image of who people thought you were.

It took me a while, but all the shenanigans and rumors had to be dissolved in my own words. God had His hand in all of this. You were only to be in my life for a season, and I am now okay with that. Thank you for your part in this script. It was well played. But I will always end up being the star of the show.

Conclusion

I wrote this memoir in total transparency and humility. The atmosphere shifted, and I had an assignment to complete. Even in my nakedness and insecurities, I wanted to be real with you. In my healing, God spoke to me and said that I must finish this and bare all, not for myself, but to help the person reading this who is struggling to heal. Death, in the end, gave me the courage to stand. It changed me. The pain changed me, and the phoenix emerged within.

God has strategically placed me in this season to carry out a mission. A mission to help heal the ones who have cried their eyes dry time and time again. To touch those hearts that have been broken or betrayed. Through it all, I have made the journey. God kept me. By His stripes, I am still standing, and the marathon continues.

Matthew 18:20

"For where two or three are gathered, in my name, there I am in the midst of them."

Ascending Affirmations

- There is a gifted purpose over your life.
- I am happy, confident, and prosperous in this season.
- God will elevate me as I serve Him.
- Where I was weak: I have been made strong.
- No devil in Hell will stop my mission to the Kingdom.
- I am at Peace.
- I have the courage to live my life to the fullest.
- I am grateful for the lessons and the blessings.
- I desire more of God's wisdom, understanding, and love.
- Every day is a new day full of hope.
- I forgive my enemies for the stones they have thrown.
- My body and mind are both healthy and strong.
- God will qualify and elevate me.
- I will achieve my dreams.
- Favor is upon me. There will be supernatural blessings and miracles.
- My heart is open to giving love and receiving love.
- There is a necessity to make a difference in the world.
- Your purpose is to make someone else's life better.
- Praise God even when you do not understand.
- You are being healed by the love of the Father.
- Declare God's promise; your season of wait is almost over.
- I am falling in love with the person God is calling me to be.

- Today, I am full of life because today is a blessing. I drink happiness and taste joy. I would not choose anything less.
- When your mind says you want to level up, enjoy life or absorb love… tell God.
- Look into the curb and lean. Stay in your lane. Keep your eyes on the destination.
- God has placed a calling over your life that you will never be able to shake.
- Let your light shine before everyone you meet.
- At times, you will have to lose the company you keep to become your radical self.
- Do not watch me fail, watch how I get up.
- Foolish pride will keep you from admitting your faults.
- Stop focusing on what you have lost. Every blessing was not meant to stay with you.
- There's power and glory from your pain.
- Nothing about your life is luck; you are favored by the "Most High."
- Pay attention to the whispers of the universe.
- Figure out your purpose and run your race.
- Everything passes in its time.
- Life has a unique way of humbling you and making you pray.
- Be in a place of appreciation so that the universe aligns you for more.
- Jump! Spread your wings! The world wants more of you.
- Awake each day and have a nice slice of humble pie. You have nothing to prove to anyone.
- Forgive yourself for the failures; then commit to investing in your passions.

- Give your dreams a chance to be birthed.
- Even through times of adversity, God's plan for you is still a perfect one.
- Scars will show in your victory to remind you of what you came through.
- For everything the enemy has stolen, God will give it back and add more.
- The Devil will no longer hold you hostage.
- Start each day with a smile. More than likely, it will end the same way… SMILING.
- BE GRATEFUL.
- Stay armored in God's Word.
- Be grateful for unlimited sources of prosperity.
- All challenges are an opportunity to evolve, be a person of positive action.
- Keep a mindset of gratitude, you will attract more prosperity.
- Celebrate the fact that you have another day alive to fulfill your dreams.
- Your smile represents a heart of gratitude.
- There is always pain before progress.
- Pain will change you; truth will enlighten you.
- Surround yourself with people that believe in you.
- Be grateful. Everything you have is by the grace of God.
- We are in a season where God will do miraculous things.
- Trust in God; there is no lack in Heaven.
- Ask God to reveal to you how His Kingdom operates.
- Make the difference you were born to make.
- Get inspired by your failures. They make you stronger and wiser.

- Your most powerful asset is your mind.
- Say to yourself, "I have already won."
- I am encouraged today that God is sending a breakthrough.
- Prepare for a mountaintop experience. God has more in store for you.
- Just when you think things couldn't get any worse, you fall right into God's grace.
- Breathe deep! Let go!
- Every journey begins with you taking the first step.
- Everything begins with a thought. Control your mind.
- You are free to soar. Lift-off!
- Just say, "God, I trust you."
- Something BIG is about to happen in your life!
- Lord, you deserve my praise.
- You are about to stumble into a breakthrough!
- Heaven has a way of just dropping blessings down at any given time.
- May God renew your strength.
- Manifest your glory by His stripes.
- Nothing shall be impossible to those who believe in God.
- God is about to expand your borders and increase your resources.
- Think bigger and receive bigger!
- God is giving you access to greater things.
- God has a strategic plan to bring you redemption.
- Good fortune is coming for you.
- God is going to openly bless you in front of your enemies.

- You have a beautiful aura.
- If you can take it, then you can make it.
- There's power in your name.
- This is your moment; you have a miracle inside of you.
- Fight harder!
- What God has spoken over your life will come to pass despite the naysayers.
- What you make happen for other people, God will make happen for you.
- God, thank you for your peace and your power.
- Gratefulness is the seed to prosperity.
- If you ever give unselfishly, your return will be multiplied.
- It is time for you to be happy!
- Sometimes you find your own healing in the process of helping others.
- Even after your hardest fall, get up again.
- The things that people say would hinder you, God will bless you.
- Whatever God removes, He restores at a higher level.
- Life is too short not to have a sense of humor.
- Hold on; God is just making some adjustments.
- I want to see you win!
- When it is your time, it is YOUR time!
- Do not allow the hurt to harden you.
- You will have favor in everything you touch.
- Love yourself first!
- Something good will happen for you today.
- A shift is coming into your life.
- Your actions speak your truth.

- Remember the ones who were down for you.
- From the time you walk out the door, your life could change instantly. Anything could happen unexpectedly. Be mindful of how you treat people and the energies you give off. Be selfless, kind, and empathetic. Be forgiving. Have a heart of gratitude and appreciation.
- Look back only to review the lessons.
- It has been a long and rough road, but God will see you through.
- Allow your heart to be selfless, and take joy from seeing other people's happiness.
- Everything you touch will prosper.
- God is moving in your direction; expect double for your troubles.
- The wait is over. You are in your season.
- The biggest blessings usually come after making many mistakes and shedding lots of tears.
- Forgiveness is for you, not for them.

Repeat these powerful and comforting affirmations daily with meditation. These positive words will change your mindset and your life!

Special Notes & Memories

Special Notes & Memories

Special Notes & Memories

Special Notes & Memories

Special Notes & Memories

About the Author

Straight out of the backwoods of Lynchburg, South Carolina. Inetta Lowery is a Luxury Realtor, Licensed Freight Broker, and owns a small logistics company. She is the prototype for all women with a huge heart for helping everyone. She is a lover of all things real estate, trucking, and God. In this memoir, Inetta plans to unapologetically help some people come out of their hurt, guilt, and grievance by sharing her own personal story. Grab your bag of popcorn and a stiff drink. You are about to get the missing pieces to this puzzle of grief and deception.